The **Small Group**
and the Vine

FOUNDATIONAL TRAINING FOR **GROUP LEADERS**

Tony Payne and
Marty Sweeney

SYDNEY · YOUNGSTOWN

Matthias Media
(St Matthias Press Ltd ACN 067 558 365)
Email: info@matthiasmedia.com.au
Internet: www.matthiasmedia.com.au
Please visit our website for current postal and telephone contact information.

Matthias Media (USA)
Email: sales@matthiasmedia.com
Internet: www.matthiasmedia.com
Please visit our website for current postal and telephone contact information.

ISBN 978 1 925424 35 5

Cover design and typesetting by Lankshear Design.

Contents

Introduction and welcome

Welcome to *The Small Group and the Vine*.

Our expectation is that you are probably new to leading a small group, and this course is your preparation for that exciting and rewarding role. But it's also possible that you might be an experienced leader who has decided to do the course as a bit of a refresh or reboot. Either way, it is good to have you along, and we hope and pray that this is a really useful investment of your time.

We want to mention a few little things before we get started:

- As you will see, in this course we use the phrase 'moving people to the right' as a shorthand way of describing the progression people make as disciples of Christ. It's a shorthand based on a diagram we use to describe how people grow as they become disciples and are transformed more and more into maturity in Christ. In our diagram, the goal is to *move people to the right*. The phrase is not intended in any way as a description of people's political leanings! We hope this isn't the case, but it could be that in your context even once you explain the intended meaning of the phrase in this course, it just has too much political baggage for you to use it as helpful shorthand. If so, you just need to use your own memorable shorthand way of talking about that process of growing people as disciples. For example, in the videos you'll notice we use 'moving towards maturity' or 'moving towards Christ' interchangeably with 'moving to the right'.
- You'll notice that we are encouraging you to do a bit of 'homework' in the form of reading Tony's book, *The Thing Is* (Matthias Media). This isn't to help Tony make some extra pocket money (he doesn't get any

royalties). It's because the book goes into more depth than we can here about the 'big picture' of what God is doing in our world, what he's doing in *people*, and the part we play in that divine plan. It's only a short book, but we think it will be a very helpful supplement to this short course. In fact, if you go to **www.matthiasmedia.com/tti.html** you'll see that we have a very special offer for you.

- We've added a whole lot of bonus input for you in the appendix section of this workbook. We hope you'll benefit from some of the articles there about the practicalities of leading a small group. Up that back end of the book we'll also tell you about some of the other resources Matthias Media has available to help you.

- We also want to acknowledge our indebtedness to Colin Marshall for his insightful thinking over many years on effective small groups, including his book *Growth Groups* (Matthias Media). If you want more guidance on your role as a small group leader, we certainly recommend his book very highly. It contains 15 very useful training topics for small group leaders, and can be used as further follow-on training for those doing this course.

- Our thanks to the many people who gave us feedback and suggestions on the course content, and special thanks to Bill Schotten for his expertise in shooting the video and attempting to make us look good on screen.

But enough of the preliminaries. Let's get on with the course.

Tony Payne and Marty Sweeney

Why *The Small Group and the Vine?*

We've called this course *The Small Group and the Vine* because in it we apply the theological convictions about Christian ministry that I (Tony) articulated with Colin Marshall in our book *The Trellis and the Vine* (Matthias Media, 2009).

In *The Trellis and the Vine* (T&V) we explain that the basic work of any Christian ministry is to preach the biblical gospel of Jesus Christ in the power of God's Spirit, and to see people converted, changed and grow to maturity in that gospel. This is where the life and power of all ministry is to be found: in the prayerful, Spirit-backed speaking of the message of the Bible by one person to another (or to more than one).

In T&V we liken this vibrant, dynamic, gospel growth to a spreading, fruitful vine, taking our cue from the imagery that Paul uses in Colossians 1:5-6. Accordingly we described the essential work of ministry—of making disciples of Jesus through the prayerful speaking of the word—as the 'vine work' that all Christians are called to take part in, each in our own way.

And just as some sort of framework or trellis is needed to help vines grow, so Christian ministries also need some structure and support. It may not be much, but at the very least we need somewhere to meet, some Bibles to read from, and some basic structures of leadership within our group. All Christian churches, fellowships and ministries have some kind of 'trellis' that gives shape and support to the work. These trellises may be administrative and managerial in nature (e.g. finances, infrastructure, organization, property, governance) or they may be 'ministry trellises' (e.g. organized groups, events, activities or meetings in which vine work can happen).

One of the very common features of church life is for 'trellises' to become too important, or to take on a life of their own, or to lose touch with their reason for existing. We forget why a particular structure or meeting or activity was set up. In fact, we can end up running trellises that don't actually facilitate much vine work at all. (This was one of T&V's significant arguments.)

Perhaps you can see why we've called this course *The Small Group and the Vine*. It's very possible—in fact, in our experience it's alarmingly common—for churches to run small groups that are like trellises on which a bedraggled vine is struggling to grow. As a structure, the group exists and runs; but it has lost focus on its central reason for being.

Our prayer is that this course will equip you to lead small groups where the vine grows and flourishes through the prayerful speaking of the word of God.

Session 1
Understanding small groups

Watch: Introduction

Read and discuss

1. In your own experience of small groups:

   a. When a small group has functioned really well, what have you appreciated about it?

   b. What sorts of things have you *not* appreciated about small groups you've been part of?

To understand what purpose God has in mind for small groups, we need to first clarify what our whole lives are about. This is because God's will for us in small groups is part of his will for us more generally—it's not some special or separate area. In other words, the task of clarifying what small groups are really all about begins with clarifying what God's big plan is for the world, and for us in particular.

2. Read Colossians 1:1-23.

   a. In verses 5-6, the gospel almost has a life of its own. What is the gospel doing?

   b. What has the gospel done or produced in the Colossians' lives (vv. 6, 12-14)?

   c. What does Paul hope and pray they will continue in/grow in (vv. 9-12)?

   d. Who is the Son? What is his place in God's plans (vv. 13-20)?

e. Based on what you've discovered so far, see if you can summarize God's will or purpose for the Colossians.

f. Read back over the whole passage again. Write down anything you find about *how* God is achieving these purposes of his. By what *means*, or through what methods, is God acting in the world?

g. What role or place do you think Christians meeting together has in what God is doing? (See Colossians 3:16, Hebrews 10:24-25.)

Watch: 'Moving to the right' in Christ

Think and discuss

1. Thinking back over what we've just seen from the Bible, what implications are there for small groups?

    a. How would you summarize in your own words the key purposes of small groups?

    b. How are those purposes achieved?

    c. How does this compare/contrast to groups you've been part of previously?

2. Have a go at crafting a short vision statement for the small group you're going to lead. Like this: "I would love to be part of a small group where we do [these things...] with the result that [this happens...]."

3. You might have noticed that the purposes we have been looking at could just as well apply to our larger Sunday gatherings.

   a. In what ways do you think small groups are similar to our main Sunday church gatherings in their purposes and in what they do to achieve those purposes? In what ways are they different?

   b. In what areas do you think small groups are particularly effective?

Watch: Conclusion

Pray

Give thanks for what God has done in Christ and for what we've seen of his amazing purposes, and pray for your understanding, trust and participation in these purposes.

Homework

We've covered lots of huge ideas in this session. To wrap your head around them, read chapters 1-3 of *The Thing Is*. (See the introduction for more about this book.)

One of the issues we had to wrestle with as we put this course together was what to call the groups we are talking about, because there are so many different names used: cell groups, home fellowships, Bible study groups, connect groups, and so on.

We've started off just using the somewhat generic term 'small groups' so that at least most people will know what we're talking about.

Now, in one sense it doesn't matter what we call them if everyone knows what we mean. But in another sense, it *does* matter—because what we call things shapes our view of them and communicates what we think and believe about their nature and purpose.

In which case, maybe 'small group' is a slightly ineffective name; it doesn't really communicate the purposes we've been looking at in this session.

We aren't going to be prescriptive with the name. But to signal that our groups have a particular goal and purpose—to move people to the right—we're going to call them 'Growth Groups' from this point on in our course. They are groups that help people grow in Christ and towards maturity in Christ, one step at a time.

The Small Group and the Vine

Session 2
Understanding your role as leader

Watch: Introduction

Read and discuss

1. What are your own expectations about leading a Growth Group?

    a. What are you looking forward to?

    b. What are you most concerned about?

c. What do you think are the key components of a Growth Group meeting?

2. Read Colossians 3:1-17.

   a. Verses 1-5 restate in slightly different words many of the ideas we looked at in session 1. See if you can represent what verses 1-5 say about the stages of the Christian life by marking and labelling key points on the arrow below:

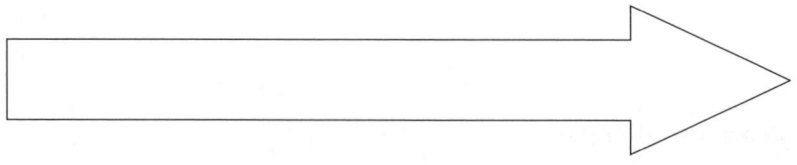

   b. Verses 5-17 go into more detail about the nature of 'transformation' to be like Christ (or 'moving to the right').

   • What does a growing maturity in Christ look like? What is it characterized by?

The Small Group and the Vine

- What one word do you think summarizes the character that we are to clothe ourselves in (or 'put on')?

- How does this transformation happen? Do you see any of the four Ps in action in this passage?

- What 'proclamation' activities are the Colossians themselves involved in (v. 16)?

- What similarities or differences do you notice between what the Colossians themselves do and what Paul does in his ministry in Colossians 1:28?

3. Read Colossians 4:2-6.

   a. Which of the four Ps do you notice in this section?

b. Who is Paul hoping will be 'moved to the right' through the clear speaking of the word of Christ?

Watch: Your role as a leader

Discuss and pray

1. How does this vision of a Growth Group leader's role make you feel? What excites you? What concerns you? What challenges you?

2. What questions do you still have?

3. If this is who you are and what your role is, how do you think this should play out in practice in your regular weekly meetings?

4. In the introductory video for this session we looked at some common views people have about the role of Growth Groups that inform their role as leaders: community-driven, service-driven, care-driven, content-driven. What is helpful about each of these views? In what ways is each deficient as a statement of the purpose of a Growth Group?[1]

5. Give thanks to God for the huge privilege of being involved with him in this work, and pray for your faithfulness and growth as you learn to do it.

Homework

We've covered lots more huge ideas in this session. To wrap your head around them, read chapters 4-6 of *The Thing Is*.

---

1   For more on this, see training topic 3 in Colin Marshall's book *Growth Groups* (see the introduction for more about this book).

Leading people to God's word

Watch: Introduction

Read and discuss
Stage 1—Understand and apply God's word to yourself

1. Read over the following explanation of the five steps that make up stage 1. Discuss in your group anything you think is unclear. Is there anything you would want to clarify or add to these steps?

    Step 1: Pray for understanding and a humble heart.
    Step 2: Read the passage and use the Swedish method or the COMA method to start working out what you think are the most significant points. (If you don't know what these methods are, see appendix 1 for a short summary.)

Step 3: Work through the pre-written questions in your Bible study, including any application questions, and make notes as you do.

Step 4: Write down what you think is the Big Point/s in a sentence or two.

Step 5: Ponder and pray over how the Big Point and other things you've noticed in the passage affect you. How is the Lord Jesus challenging you through this word? How is he challenging the way you think, and the way you act? What should you repent of? What do you need to embrace and trust? Love means you should do... what?

2. Now let's do a short example of these five steps together.

Step 1: Pray for understanding and a humble heart.

Step 2: Read Hebrews 10:19-25, and use the Swedish or COMA method to get a sense of what is going on in the passage.

Step 3: Now work through the following five questions (i.e. as if this was the pre-written Bible study you were using):

a. What has God already done and promised in Jesus Christ?

b. How does this generate a 'hope' that we confess?

c. Why do you think persevering or 'holding fast' in this confession is difficult?

d. What sort of life flows from having this hope?

e. What does this mean for Christians meeting together?

Step 4: Now see if you can summarize in one sentence the Big Point or main idea of Hebrews 10:19-25.

Step 5: What aspects of this passage and its Big Point particularly challenge you or apply to you personally?

Stage 2—Prepare to lead others to God's word

If you were writing your own Bible study,[2] you would now work out what questions you want to ask your group members to help them get to the main point of the passage and apply it to themselves—that is, to take them on the same journey of discovery you have just been on yourself.

But given that you're using a pre-written study to start off with, here are six steps you might take in preparing to use the study questions you have in front of you to lead your group to the Word.

If you have time now, you could work through these steps in relation to the Hebrews 10:19-25 questions above (in step 3 under stage 1). If you are short of time, you could break the training group up into six subgroups and look at one step each (1 to 6), then share your thoughts with the whole group. Alternatively, you could all do this exercise at home and share your thoughts before the next session (session 4).

Step 1:   Is the opening question or discussion point one that would work for your group, and get conversation started? If not, how would you modify it? Or can you think of another way to lead into the discussion?

Step 2:   Do any of the questions strike you as difficult for the group to answer? How would you clarify the question? Or what supplementary question might you ask to help the group out?

2   The COMA Bible reading framework explained in appendix 1 is a useful starting point for learning how to do this. But for more detailed guidance on preparing your own Bible studies, see training topic 5 in Colin Marshall's book *Growth Groups*, and Richard Sweatman's short guide to preparing a Bible study, *Writing a Small Group Study* (Matthias Media).

Step 3: Which do you think are the really key questions—the ones that really get you towards the destination? And correspondingly, are there any that you could skip over if you were short of time? Are there any questions you could helpfully add?

Step 4: Are there any points where you might want to provide a little key summary of where you've got to, to keep the group on track to where you're going? If so, write a sentence or two that you could use.

Step 5:   Are the application questions adequate? Do they help the group to discuss their response to the passage and its main point? Are there questions you'd skip, or others you'd like to emphasize or add in—for example, that specifically apply to your context as a group, or that come out of your own application of the passage to yourself (in stage 1)?

Step 6:   Are there any particularly sensitive issues or touchy subjects in the passage/study that you need to spend some extra time thinking about how to handle? Both in terms of subject matter (sexuality, grief, etc.) and in terms of what someone in the group is dealing with (loss of job, sick parent/child, marriage problems, etc.).

As you do all this, you'll end up with your own personalized 'working version' of the pre-written study; with notes and summaries jotted here and there; with key questions underlined or extra supplementary questions written in; with notes to yourself about what to emphasize; and so on.

Watch: Stage 3—Lead the discussion

Discuss and pray

1. Of the three stages of preparing a Bible study, which one do you think you will find most challenging/difficult?

2. Pray about these challenges and also about some of things you saw in Hebrews 10.

Homework

Read chapters 7-9 of *The Thing Is*.

Session 4
Leading in prayer

Watch: Introduction

Read and discuss

1. Read Colossians 1:3-14.

    a. What motivates Paul to pray for the Colossians?

    b. What things does he pray for in verses 9-10? What outcomes does he hope for?

c. What things does he pray for in verses 11-12? What outcomes does he hope for?

d. How do you think thanksgiving relates to prayer?

e. How do you think Paul's prayers relate to "the word of truth"/"the gospel"?

f. How would you describe the part that prayer plays in Paul's ministry?

2. What has been your own experience of prayer in Growth Groups you've been part of?

   a. The good?

   b. The not-so-good?

3. How does Paul's practice of prayer and the content of his prayers challenge or encourage you with respect to prayer in Growth Groups? What can we learn from him?

Watch: The what, why and how of prayer

Discuss and pray

1. Which of the points mentioned in the video struck you as particularly useful in promoting a healthy group prayer life?[3]

2. Spend some time praying about prayer:

    *   Pray about our weakness and tendency to give up on prayer.
    *   Pray about our frequent self-centeredness (rather than God-centeredness) in prayer.
    *   Ask God to so fill us with his wisdom and understanding, and so strengthen us by his power, that we would flourish as pray-ers and persevere in praying over time.

---

3   For further ideas on how to make prayer more a part of your group, and for very practical help in actually putting it into practice, check out appendices 6, 7 and 8 of this workbook; training topic 8 in Colin Marshall's book *Growth Groups*; and articles and tips in *The Growth Group Notebook* (for more information about this resource, see the end of this workbook).

Session 5
Persevering with people

Watch: Introduction

Read and discuss

1. Read 1 Thessalonians 2:1-12.

   a. How does Paul feel about the Thessalonians?

   b. When he was with them, how was this expressed in his ministry to them? What words are used to describe what he did for them and with them?

2. Now read 1 Thessalonians 2:17-3:10.

   a. What was Paul's main worry about the Thessalonians?

   b. How is Paul's concern for them revealed in his actions?

   c. What does Paul's reaction to the news about the Thessalonians reveal about his relationship with them?

3. Now read 1 Thessalonians 5:11-15.

   a. What words are used to describe the ministry of the Thessalonian believers to one another?

   b. How does this compare to:

   • Paul's ministry to them (back in chapter 2)?

   • the ministry of the leaders of the Thessalonian church?

Watch: It's all about people

Think and discuss

1. Think about groups you've been in, and about the material on 'People' in this session. What strikes you as particularly important to work on in:

    a. getting to know and caring for the people in your group as the leader?

    b. helping your group get to know each other, and start to love and care for each other?

2. Share some ideas for how to help group members get to know each other and encourage/care for each other.

3. Discuss specific actions you can take as a group to support each other as you set out on (or continue in) the role of leading Growth Groups.

Watch: The first 8 weeks and beyond

Pray

Pray about all that you have learned in this session and through the course as a whole. Pray for yourselves as leaders and models of what it looks like to be people who are moving to the right and helping others to do likewise.

Two simple frameworks for Bible reading
By David Helm and Tony Payne

As you will soon pick up, the following article was actually written to help people read the Bible well in a one-to-one context. The two frameworks it outlines, however, are useful for any type of Bible reading and study.

Many people have found the following two methods or frameworks for reading the Bible very helpful, especially in getting started. When you're new to one-to-one Bible reading, using one of these frameworks often just helps you to get into the text and start mining its riches.

1. The Swedish method
This is a very simple, baby-steps framework for people who feel insecure about their ability to start doing one-to-one Bible reading. You could start out with this approach (perhaps for a while) and then move on to the more substantial COMA method (see below) when you have a bit of confidence going.

This simple way of reading the Bible was apparently popularized by Ada Lum, a staff worker with the International Fellowship of Evangelical Students. She named it after the Swedish student group where she first saw it used. It goes like this:

1. Read the passage aloud.
2. Each person then reads back over the passage on their own, and looks for three things:

 A light bulb: anything that shines out in the passage and draws attention; it can be something important, or something that particularly strikes the reader.

 A question mark: anything that is hard to understand; something that the reader would like to be able to ask the author about.

 An arrow: anything that applies personally to the reader's life.

3. Each person should write down at least one thing and no more than three under each category. If you are preparing for your one-to-one meeting in advance, then this constitutes the preparation. Each person should come to the meeting with at least one light bulb, one question mark, and one arrow from the passage.

   If you are not preparing, you will need to allow some time for each of you to read back through the passage and write down your light bulb, question mark and arrow. You will need to allow 5-10 minutes for this, depending on the length of the passage.
4. You each share your light bulb/s, and discuss.
5. You each share your question mark/s, and then do your best to work out answers together from the passage (although it doesn't matter if you can't find an answer).
6. You each share your arrow/s, and discuss.
7. You pray together about what you have learned.

As you gain confidence and grow in your familiarity with the Bible, you could expand the range of things you look for or consider as you read the passage. For example, you could look for the central idea of the passage (using a heart symbol); or you could write down the names of people who might benefit if you shared with them what you've learned (using a speech bubble symbol), with the aim of talking with those people before your next meeting. It's really up to you as to how much you vary and expand the basic method.

The great strength of the Swedish method is its simplicity. It's a very effective way to get started in reading the Bible together, particularly with people who are new to the Bible or who lack confidence in their ability to read the Bible for themselves.

2. The COMA method

As you get more experienced in Bible reading, or if you are meeting with someone who is already a reasonably solid Christian, you will no doubt find that you want to push a little further in understanding the passage. The COMA method is a superb tool for one-to-one Bible reading, both because of its flexibility and because it helps people to integrate their personal Bible reading with the bigger picture of the Bible—the unfolding story of Jesus Christ's saving rulership. As a result, this method helps people to avoid common pitfalls in understanding the Bible. And while it is much more substantial than the Swedish method, the COMA method can still be used easily by people who are not used to looking at a Bible text in any depth.

COMA stands for:

Context
Observation
Meaning
Application

This is really a summary of how we read anything. Even when we pick up a newspaper article, we notice what sort of thing we are reading and how it fits with other things around it (context); we read the words and sentences and paragraphs, taking note of the main events, people and content (observation); we integrate what we've observed in our heads and form a conclusion about what the author is trying to say (meaning); and we reflect on whether the author's message has any relevance for our lives (application).

It can be very useful to follow the COMA process consciously when we read the Bible, because it encourages us to ask good questions of the text and to understand it clearly and thoroughly. When we're reading one-to-one, it also very helpfully directs the conversation. You can work through the four steps together and come to some conclusions, rather than bouncing around with lots of different random thoughts or observations.

A one-to-one Bible reading meeting using the COMA method would go like this:

1. Read the passage aloud.
2. You ask some **context** questions of the text:
   - What sort of writing is this? (A letter, a narrative, a poem?)
   - Are there any clues about the circumstances under which it was written?
   - What has happened so far?
3. You ask some **observation** questions of the text:
   - Are there any major sub-sections or breaks in the text?
   - What is the main point or points?
   - What surprises are there?
   - What are the key words? What words or ideas are repeated?
4. You ask some **meaning** questions of the text:
   - How does this text relate to other parts of the book?
   - How does the passage relate to Jesus?
   - What does this teach us about God?
   - How could we sum up the meaning of this passage in our own words?
5. You ask some **application** questions of the text:
   - How does this passage challenge (or confirm) my understanding?
   - Is there some attitude I need to change?
   - How does this passage call on me to change the way I live?
6. You pray together about what you have learned.

One of the real strengths of the COMA approach to Bible reading is that it is so easily applicable to the many different genres of literature that we find in the Bible—Gospels, letters, narratives, poetry, prophecy, proverbs, and so on. (For help with adapting the COMA questions for each of the major literary genres we find in the Bible, see chapter 10 of *One-to-One Bible Reading* by David Helm.)

———◆———

Reproduced with permission from chapter 8 of *One-to-One Bible Reading: A Simple Guide for Every Christian* by David Helm (Matthias Media, Sydney, 2011).

How to be in a small group
By Tony Payne

Another year, another Bible study group. Time to sign up, turn up and get things rolling. Ho hum.

Time also perhaps to ask some questions about your own contribution to the small group you are in. Are you making much of a difference in the lives of your fellow group members? Do you feel as if you just go along because that's what you're expected to do? What part are *you* going to play in this year's group?

Why go in the first place?
People go to small groups for all sorts of reasons—to fulfil expectations, to make friends, to pursue romantic possibilities, to receive encouragement and counsel, to learn, and so on.

While most of these might be perfectly acceptable reasons to join a small group, the first and indispensable reason must be clear in our minds. Our primary reason for belonging to a small group is *to give us opportunity to love and encourage other people in Christ*. It's not about Me; it's about Them. And it's about Them because of Christ.

This, after all, is what the Christian life is about. We are commanded to love other people as Christ has loved us—to lay down our lives for them as Christ did for us. This applies as much to small groups as it does to marriages, families, workplaces and larger Christian meetings. We go to small groups not primarily to have our needs met, but to meet the needs of others. Of course, we have needs too, and no doubt they will be met along the way, but we can let others worry about that. In fact, paradoxically, the more we focus on loving others and doing whatever we can for them, the more encouragement and strength we find ourselves.

There are many ways we can love and encourage the other people in our groups. Here are five powerful ones (complete with alliterative titles).

1. The power of presence

This is the simplest and most obvious way, but it is no less powerful for being so. Just being there each week without fail is a powerful encouragement to the other members of the group. In making the group time a solid commitment, to be missed only in times of emergency, you send a very clear message to the other members: "Being with you matters very much to me. Unless something very important comes up, you can expect me. Encouraging you is a top priority."

Conversely, inconsistent attendance sends a somewhat less encouraging message: "I don't mind coming, but it's not that important. If I feel a bit tired or something else crops up, don't expect me. Being with you and encouraging you isn't really a very high priority for me."

2. The power of preparation

Most small groups complete their evening's Bible study with a plaintive plea from the leader for people to read the passage and prepare for next week's study. The leader knows full well that most people won't, but there's no harm in trying!

However, preparing for the group time is another powerful way to love the members of the group. Of course, having read the passage or done the homework greatly increases the benefit you yourself receive from the discussion. More importantly, however, *it equips you to encourage others* by what you say. Rather than throwing in whatever occurs to you at the time, you have actually thought about the Bible passage and the issues that it raises. You are much better prepared to say things that stimulate, encourage and teach others.

3. The power of prayer

Paul's friend and fellow worker, Epaphras, would have made an ideal small group member. According to Paul, he was always "struggling on [the Colossians'] behalf in his prayers", that they might "stand mature and fully assured in all the will of God". Paul was able to vouch that, in doing so, Epaphras had "worked hard for [the Colossians]" (Col 4:12-13).

Praying for others is hard work, but real work. It is one of the most loving things we can do for our fellow group members, because God will work in people's lives in answer to our prayers. It may be a quiet, inconspicuous form of ministry but, in God's eyes, it is a precious one, and his approval is what matters.

4. The power of personality

The alliteration may be starting to stretch a little thin here, but the point is solid enough—that a powerful way of loving others in your small group is to be willing to share your own life and personality with them.

This is by no means an easy thing to do. Many of us would much rather keep quiet and not give too much away. However, by opening up and sharing our lives and thoughts, struggles and joys, we do others a great service. We not only show them that we have the very same struggles that they have (but thought they were alone in suffering), we also encourage them to open up as well.

Of course, it is anything but loving to indiscriminately dump everything we are thinking or feeling onto the group. We need to heed the advice of Proverbs (e.g. Prov 12:18) as well as the words of Ephesians 4: "Let no corrupting talk come out of your mouths, but only such as is good for building up, as fits the occasion, that it may give grace to those who hear" (Eph 4:29).

5. The power of love

Whatever you do in the group—every word you say, every action—do it for the sake of others. Look for how you can support and help the leader. Look for ways to care for the members of the group—those who could really do with a phone call or visit; those who would benefit from having someone to pray or read the Bible with; those who need financial or other material help; those who just need a friend to come over for pizza and a movie.

Belonging to a small group can be a very demanding exercise. In fact, it can cost us our lives, because that is what it means to be a follower of Christ—to lay down our lives for the sake of others. If we grasp the possibilities, small groups represent an enormously fruitful opportunity for doing just that.

You can download this article as a nicely formatted PDF **for emailing or printing for your group members:**
- www.bit.ly/htbiasgA4 (A4 size)
- www.bit.ly/htbiasgUS (US letter size)

Originally published in *The Briefing* and reproduced here with permission. Available online: www.matthiasmedia.com/briefing/2006/02/how-to-be-a-small-group-member/

Appendix 3
How to use pre-written Bible studies
By Richard Sweatman

Are pre-written Bible studies the microwave dinners of Growth Group ministry? For busy leaders it sometimes feels that way. No preparation required: the study is ready to go in the time it takes to hand out the booklets, and all the good stuff within is the result of someone else's hard work.

Now that approach to using pre-written studies might be familiar to us, but is it good? Haven't our consciences protested against our laziness in those times? Have we really been "rightly handling the word of truth" (2 Tim 2:15)?

Pre-written studies have a place in Growth Group leading, but they work best when we use them to teach the Bible well rather than just to save time. Whether they are the work of your own pastor or an off-the-shelf product, the following guidelines will help you use them faithfully and effectively.

Begin by setting aside some time a few days or a week before you lead the study. This will allow you to ruminate on the study and come up with improvements or creative ideas. Take a moment to pray for your group members and for God's help in preparing the study.

For exegetical studies (i.e. studies based on a Bible passage) open your Bible and have a close look at the passage before you even look at the study. Ask yourself the following questions:
- Where does the passage fit in the book?
- What is the passage saying?
- What do I think it means?

- How does the passage fit with Jesus and the gospel?
- How should we apply the passage?

For topical studies (i.e. studies that focus on a doctrine or theme in the Bible) your approach needs to be a bit different. Take a blank piece of paper and your Bible and have a think about these questions:
- What questions do I have about the topic?
- What Bible passages would I look up to understand it better?
- What connection does this topic have with other doctrines (for example, creation, sin, God's character)?
- How does the cross affect the way I understand it?
- What applications might a study on this include?

You'll find answering some of these questions pretty hard (you can be sure the study writer found them hard too) but the process will get you thinking and lead to a more engaging study in the end. Don't stress if you can't think of answers to the questions in the time you have—the whole idea of a pre-written study is for it to be a help for you!

The next step in preparing a pre-written study (whether exegetical or topical) is to do the study yourself. Try not to be too critical at this point; think of the process as a spiritual exercise and apply what you learn to your own life. As you learn and grow you'll find yourself looking forward to sharing the same experience with your group.

After running through the study yourself, have a look at the leader's notes (if provided). This step will help you with two things. Firstly, you will learn more and find things you missed on your initial run through. Secondly, you can assess how well the study works. Are the questions written so that they draw out the hoped-for answers? Would extra questions be helpful? If you have time, and you still have questions about a passage, this would be when you would look up verses in a commentary.

The final step is, in a sense, to make the study your own. Think about the group and look at the study again. How long should you plan for each question? Are there any questions you need to rephrase? Which questions might you skip if you are short on time? Are there extra questions that would help draw out the teaching goals or applications? Is there a tangent you should go down that is particularly relevant for your group? Is there something creative you could bring to the study? Write down all the changes and notes you need. This is now your study. You are ready to go, and hopefully looking forward to the gathering!

Does that process sound as easy as cooking a microwave dinner? Obviously, no! But will the hard work benefit your group? Emphatically, yes. Under God, your prayerful and thoughtful preparation will help people grow and change in response to his Word. Why not commit to making your next pre-written study your best yet?

Originally published at *GoThereFor.com* and reproduced here with permission. Available online: www.gotherefor.com/offer.php?intid=29761

Help your home group grow closer together
By Tara Sing

Home groups start off as a bunch of strangers gathering together to read the Bible, but the hope is that they will grow to be more. Our ideal home groups are places where people care for one another, they are open and honest with each other, and they do life together. However, getting from being a bunch of strangers to being buddies can be difficult, and so it is worth thinking through how you will develop a group culture amongst your group members.

Here are some suggestions for helping the people in your group grow closer together.

Spend time having fun together
God needs to be at the centre of your relationships, but that doesn't mean that you can't have fun together. Sometimes common experiences outside of the normal Bible study framework can help a group to gel. The Bible is still the focus of your friendships, but they've had the chance to also develop in a different context.

Get your hands dirty together
People bond over shared experiences and nothing says 'shared experience' like getting together and getting your hands dirty. Your group might like to volunteer to be on the church cleaning roster, or you might like to organize

a way for your group to help set up or pack up for a church event. There are usually many different ways for groups to help out at church. If you're feeling stuck for ideas, why not brainstorm in your group different ways that you can serve together and different things you can work on.

Share the gospel together

One of the lovely things about joining a short-term mission team is the relationships you form with one another as you pray together and share the gospel with others. But you don't need to join a short-term mission to help those in your group grow closer together. You may like to do some local evangelism together, perhaps giving away evangelistic books or tracts.

Grow your church together

It can be very easy for a group to become inward focused. It's worth thinking through how you can be encouraging your group to think about the wider church together, and how they can help their church grow both in number and in faith. A great way to help your home group become outward focused is to spend time together thinking about how you can serve the wider church. *Six Steps to Loving Your Church* (Matthias Media) is designed especially for this purpose, helping groups to look at their attitudes towards church, what the Bible says about the purpose of church, what it means to love your church and the people who go there, and how everyone can be engaged in loving service before, during and after the Sunday service.

Ultimately, the goal of your home group is not to be best buddies, but to be growing in faith. We want our home groups and our Bible studies to be places where Jesus is the focus and the main priority. It is a good thing to help our group members get to know one another and build good relationships with each other, but we mustn't forget that our priority must be growing in our relationship with God.

———————◆———————

Originally published at *GoThereFor.com* and reproduced here with permission. Available online: www.gotherefor.com/offer.php?intid=28575

Ezra and the principle of de-termination

By Ian Carmichael

The other day I came across this interesting snippet about Ezra:

> Now Ezra had determined in his heart to study the law of the LORD, obey it, and teach its statutes and ordinances in Israel. (Ezra 7:10, HCSB)

Ezra made a resolution to become a student of the word, to personally obey it, and to teach it to others.

Ezra is a helpful illustration of the way that God works in his world. The word of God is received, and by the power of God's Spirit the word does its work in the heart and mind of the believer. But although the word will "dwell in [us] richly", the expectation is that it does not get locked up in us; it is shared and passed on to others (Col 3:16).

The inward, life-changing movement of God's word is vital in the life of every Christian. It is nicely captured in the famous prayer of Thomas Cranmer: "Blessed Lord, who hast caused all holy Scriptures to be written for our learning; grant that we may in such wise hear them, read, mark, learn, and inwardly digest them..."[4]

But the outward movement of God's word is also an important theme of

---

4   Recorded in the 1662 Book of Common Prayer.

the Bible. Not only do we 'inwardly digest' it, but the expectation is that we will pass on what we learn to others, and so the word of God will spread and grow (Ps 78:1-7; Matt 13:23; Acts 6:7; Rom 15:14; 1 Cor 14:26; Col 1:6; 1 Pet 2:9). As one of my friends puts it, "The word of God isn't meant to terminate with me".

Perhaps Cranmer's prayer might helpfully be changed to "hear, read, mark, learn, inwardly digest, and share" the Scriptures.

Leading a home group is one way of sharing the Scriptures, as is preaching a sermon or giving a talk. But these are certainly not the only ways, and perhaps it would be helpful to remind the members of our group—who are not preachers or home group leaders—that there are many other ways that they can share the Scriptures too.

Actually, this principle—that the word of God isn't meant to terminate with me—is the core principle that helps home groups to become disciple-making teams, because it is the prayerful spreading of the word of God that makes disciples.

So I want to suggest that there should be three key questions at the end of every group Bible study:

- What have we learned?
- How should we pray and change in response to what we've learned?
- Who can we prayerfully share what we've learned with and how?

The answer to that third question may be as simple as this: "When I get home, and my flatmate asks me how Bible study was, instead of saying just 'Good, thanks', I'm going to say 'Good thanks. I was reminded that...'"

Or it might be: "I'm going to send an email to a missionary to encourage them with the truth that..."

Or: "I'm going to figure out how I can simplify what I've learned and teach it to my children over dinner tomorrow night."

Or, for those who are a bit braver: "I'm going to look for a way to share that truth with Jeff at the office, even though he's not a Christian, because I think it would really help him to think about that."

Of course, considering how I might pass what I've learned on to others should not replace the vital question of how I might personally need to change in response to God's word. But the process of working out how to pass it on can actually really help in internalizing what you've learned and be a useful prompt to implementing those needed personal changes.

So put the challenge to your group: "Let's make sure we're Christians of de-termination".

Appendix 6
Prayer in the small group
By Tony Payne

What follows is a set of notes that formed the basis of a training presentation for home group leaders.

1. How or what?

- When we turn to the Bible, we find very little on the nuts and bolts of how to pray. Nothing much on posture, on length of time, on when and where, on the rituals that should accompany it, and so on.

- We do find some important indications of how: such as that prayer is always verbal—words; that it is conducted with a humble confidence in our access to God's throne, as his sons; that it takes place by and in the work of the Spirit in us; that we should pray through Jesus the Son to the Father; and that we should accompany our prayers with thanksgivings for all the benefits and blessings we receive.

- But very little is given on the detail. No precise formula or technique. Which may disappoint us—but shouldn't surprise us. It's about a relationship with God not a technique! And this should also delight us, not only because a personal relationship is so much better than a mechanical manipulation through certain techniques, but because of the freedom! We can pray in all sorts of ways and times and places. In all sorts of circumstances. Everywhere and at all times.

- Interestingly, when the disciples ask Jesus to teach them to pray, he doesn't give them instructions on the technique of how to pray, so much as telling them *what to pray.*

- In fact, the *how* of prayer in the Bible is largely the same as the *what.*
- And this is largely the problem for us and for our groups as well, is it not? *What* to pray for!
- The typical small group: you get to the prayer time, and go round the group for prayer points—wise use of time; my quiet time; work, which is stressful; sickness; little hassles of life; some trouble that has come up (e.g. family problems); etc. You want it to be better than this—but you still want to be able to share and pray for anything.

Here's a helpful way to think about it. The **desires of God** and the **anxieties of life...**

2. The desires of God

"If you then, who are evil, know how to give good gifts to your children, how much more will your Father who is in heaven give good things to those who ask him!" (Matt 7:11)

Our heavenly Father is more than willing to give us good things—but what are the good things he wants to give us? If we knew that, we could pray with great confidence, and expect him to answer in the affirmative.

In other words, if we knew what was on God's agenda, what his will for us was, what his priorities and plans were—what his desires for us were— then those should surely dominate our prayers.

How would we discover the desires of God, the things that he really wants to give us?

There are several ways.

a. Look at his revealed plans

First we should thank our Father that we are not in the dark as to his plans; as to what he's doing; what his 'to do' list is. It's revealed in the gospel of Jesus Christ, and in the New Testament that teaches it.

- We could look at Bible passages like Ephesians 1:1-14, which majestically summarizes what God is up to in the world—that from before the foundation of the world he has been working to save and redeem and adopt as his own sons his chosen people, that they might be united together under one head, Christ. In fact, this is his big goal for everything: that everything in heaven and earth be united under Christ.

- Or 1 Thessalonians 5:23-24: "Now may the God of peace himself sanctify you completely, and may your whole spirit and soul and body be kept blameless at the coming of our Lord Jesus Christ. He who calls you is faithful; he will surely do it."
- Or 2 Thessalonians 1:11-12: "To this end we always pray for you, that our God may make you worthy of his calling and may fulfil every resolve for good and every work of faith by his power, so that the name of our Lord Jesus may be glorified in you, and you in him, according to the grace of our God and the Lord Jesus Christ." God's desire is that the Lord Jesus be glorified in everything we do: in our daily walk, in every work of faith.
- Or Matthew 6:25-34: God's priority is the kingdom; that's what's really important, so we should seek that first, rather than running around stressing about what to eat or what to wear.
- By looking at these and similar Bible passages, we can see what is on God's heart; what he works and plans for; and what he is always willing and ready to do in our own lives if we would ask him.

b. Look at his promises

We can see much the same thing by looking at his many wonderful promises, which show what he wants to give, and guarantees that he will give us. When God gives a clear promise, then we can call upon him to fulfil it.

- Romans 10:13: "For 'everyone who calls on the name of the Lord will be saved'."
- Acts 10:43: "To him all the prophets bear witness that everyone who believes in him receives forgiveness of sins through his name."
- 1 Corinthians 10:13: "No temptation has overtaken you that is not common to man. God is faithful, and he will not let you be tempted

beyond your ability, but with the temptation he will also provide the way of escape, that you may be able to endure it."

- James 1:5: "If any of you lacks wisdom, let him ask God, who gives generously to all without reproach, and it will be given him."
- And so on, and so forth. We can pray the promises of God with confidence. And indeed we should.

c. Look at his commands

- We can also pray confidently for the things that God commands, because we know that he obviously wants those things to happen. In commanding something, he reveals his will, his desires, his agenda.
- So pray the Ten Commandments. Pray for God's Spirit to write these onto your heart in their New Covenant application, and lead you to do them.
- Or take a passage such as this:

> Therefore be imitators of God, as beloved children. And walk in love, as Christ loved us and gave himself up for us, a fragrant offering and sacrifice to God.
>
> But sexual immorality and all impurity or covetousness must not even be named among you, as is proper among saints. Let there be no filthiness nor foolish talk nor crude joking, which are out of place, but instead let there be thanksgiving. (Eph 5:1-4)

There's about a week's worth of quiet times right there—those things God is wanting and indeed commanding us to do, and which we struggle to do.

d. Look at the prayers of Scripture

You want to know what God really wants you to pray for, and which he longs to give you? Look at all the templates he has given you, the examples of godly prayer that are full of God's desires and will:

- Look at the prayers of Jesus in John 17 and Mark 14.
- Look at the prayers of Paul, especially the magnificent ones at the

The Small Group and the Vine

opening of Colossians and Philippians, and about half way through Ephesians.

- Or look at the prayers of the OT saints in Nehemiah 9, Daniel 9 or David's prayers in the psalms, such as Psalm 51.
- Perhaps most of all, look at the model prayer that Jesus gave us: the Lord's Prayer. Note how focused the prayer is on the coming kingdom, and on the work of that kingdom in the world now. Use the Lord's Prayer as a model for your prayers—mull over each petition, and expand it into prayers for all manner of things.

e. Pray the Scriptures

Any passage of Scripture will reveal God's mind to us, and shape our prayers.

- See Luther's book written for his barber: *A Simple Way to Pray*.
- Luther read the Lord's Prayer, the Ten Commandments, or indeed any psalm or part of Scripture and after considering what it is that the Scripture is instructing or urging or teaching, he turned it into: a thanksgiving, a confession, a prayer.
- Take the little passage in 1 Corinthians 1:10-17. Read it, and show how it can be a thanksgiving, a confession and a prayer.
- This is a great model for personal prayer—but obviously also for our small groups. Study a passage, and then pray it together. Find things to thank God for, to confess and to pray—for each other and for others.

3. The anxieties of life

And so we are instructed in the desires of God, and these should shape and dominate our prayers.

But what of those things about which the Bible is silent? The things that happen to us day by day? What we might call the anxieties of life?

Well, the Bible is not silent about them either. It tells us that we should bring them to God. Quite clear: "do not be anxious about anything, but in everything by prayer and supplication with thanksgiving let your requests be made known to God" (Phil 4:6).

So how do we do this? What do we pray for in these circumstances?

a. With a Christian mind

The way we think about things will reflect our renewed mind. Becoming a Christian involves a change of mind—not just decisively in rejecting the big lie of independence and idolatry, and embracing the truth of God and Christ —but an ongoing transformation of our mind.

> Do not be conformed to this world, but be transformed by the renewal of your mind, that by testing you may discern what is the will of God, what is good and acceptable and perfect. (Rom 12:2)

> Finally, brothers, whatever is true, whatever is honourable, whatever is just, whatever is pure, whatever is lovely, whatever is commendable, if there is any excellence, if there is anything worthy of praise, think about these things. (Phil 4:8)

The way we pray for things, the way we approach the troubles and issues and anxieties of life, will be shaped by how much our Christian mind has developed—that is, how much our thoughts, beliefs, and knowledge have been transformed so as to reflect God's mind.

And so, for example, when we pray for someone who is sick or undergoing trial:

- Pray not just for their healing and deliverance but because we've come to appreciate that godliness and holiness, being transformed into the likeness of our Saviour, is ultimately more important than health or ease or comfort, we'll also pray that the person be transformed through the experience.
- But because we'll never know fully, and never be fully renewed this side of glory, we should still pray 'if it be thy will' when God hasn't revealed what he wants us to pray for.
- If he has revealed his will (e.g. don't commit adultery), then it's pointless and grossly disobedient and faithless to pray, "Lord, I'm not sure whether you want me to commit adultery with Jack, and I'm not sure what the right thing to do is, but I commit this to you, 'Your will be done!'"
- But when God hasn't revealed or promised us something, we have to

leave it in his sovereign care. I was taught that "If it be thy will" was a faithless unbelieving prayer! Strange, since it was the Lord's prayer (Luke 22:42)!

b. None too big or small

The second thing to note:

- No anxiety about anything (Phil 4:6).
- We can and should pour out all our anxieties and worries before our Father, because he cares for us: "Humble yourselves, therefore, under the mighty hand of God so that at the proper time he may exalt you, casting all your anxieties on him, because he cares for you" (1 Pet 5:6-7).
- Nothing too small (hairs on head).
- Nothing too big (is anything impossible with God?).

c. With thanksgiving

Thirdly, as we pour them out, it's with thanksgiving: "...do not be anxious about anything, but in everything by prayer and supplication with thanksgiving let your requests be made known to God" (Phil 4:6).

Not only is it positive and uplifting to our anxious spirits to remember all that God has blessed us with and give thanks to him—not only does it refocus our minds on the goodness of God and stop us feeling sorry for ourselves—but also it's a further expression of trust: that we know that God will do what's best for us, even when we don't know what to pray. And so we thank him.

d. God knows

The fourth and final thing to remember when we're praying about life's suffering and anxieties, and aren't even sure what to pray for, is that God knows us, and dwells with us, and understands even better than we do what is going on.

I think that's the meaning of those enigmatic verses in Romans 8:

Likewise the Spirit helps us in our weakness. For we do not know what to pray for as we ought, but the Spirit himself intercedes for us with groanings too deep for words. And he who searches hearts knows what is the mind of the Spirit, because the Spirit intercedes for the saints according to the will of God. (vv. 26-27)

This doesn't say that the Spirit tells us what to pray for, or even that he edits or fixes up our prayers, like a filter, and sends them off to God in better shape. Simply that God by his own Spirit dwells within us, and so God speaks to God on our behalf.

4. Practical suggestions

So in terms of your small groups, what you want to do is:

- Make sure your prayers focus on the desires of God, not just your own anxieties, troubles and trivial concerns.
- At the same time, allow room for anxieties, troubles and trivial concerns to be brought before the Father who cares for us in everything, with thanksgiving.

As a regular pattern each week, try the pattern of Luther. His barber asked him how to pray. After the passage, ask: From this passage...

- What can we give thanks for?
- What sin should we confess?
- What does it tell us about the desires of God to inform our prayers? The things God really wants us to pray for?

And then pray. And then ask:

- Are there are any other anxieties or troubles or concerns that people want to bring before God?

And pray again. Which of course means leaving enough time to pray! Try to vary it—have one week a month that concentrates on prayer:

- Take a week where you don't have a long study but simply read a classic passage, and then ask Luther's three questions, and then spend quite some time in prayer.
- Then break into smaller groups of three for sharing particular causes of thanksgiving, anxieties and praying.

Start the evening with prayer. Talk about troubles and anxieties at the start: have each person share one thanksgiving and one anxiety—and then pray. And pray again after the Bible study for matters that arise from the study.

Appendix 7
More thoughts about prayer in small groups
By Ian Carmichael

Continue steadfastly in prayer, being watchful in it with thanksgiving.
(Col 4:2)

This verse appears at the top of the weekly prayer list we use at our team meetings at Matthias Media. Why? Well, sometimes prayer seems like a joy. But quite often it doesn't; it feels like hard work and it is tempting to skip it. That's why Colossians 4:2 is such a useful reminder.

It's not a difficult verse to understand, is it? But let me make a few observations I hope might help us in applying it to our home groups.

"Continue steadfastly"
These words imply that significant effort is required to keep praying. As Peter O'Brien puts it (in his Word Biblical Commentary): "Here the injunction suggests determination in prayer, with the resolve not to give up (Luke 11:5-13) or grow weary (Luke 18:1-8)".[5]

I'm glad to say that prayer seems to be a pretty fixed item on the weekly agenda of our home groups—and thankfully I've not really heard of any groups ending up not praying at all. But nonetheless it is easy for prayer to

---

5   Peter O'Brien, *Colossians-Philemon*, Word Biblical Commentary, vol. 44, Thomas Nelson, Dallas, 2002, p. 238.

become brief and superficial. Or for it to get squeezed out because the Bible study goes a bit long and we're all getting a bit tired.

God is calling on us to make prayer a priority, so maybe that means praying *before* the Bible study sometimes. (But be disciplined and don't squeeze out hearing from God's word regularly either.) And maybe, for you as leader, it means putting preparation into the prayer time just like you do for the study time, so that you can lead people in 'watchful' and 'thankful' prayer.

"in prayer"

What we are to continue in is *prayer*—not collecting up prayer points! Too often we spend more time in our home groups going around the room sharing prayer points than we do *actually praying* to our heavenly Father. Although giving people the chance to share personal concerns is important, so is praying together. With a little bit of thought, both are possible. Here are a few suggestions:

- Set up an online weekly prayer point register[6] and send an email or SMS reminder for group members to add their prayer points before you meet together. Then print off the list for everyone and pass it round at the group, giving people a few minutes to read through and ask any questions. The advantage of this is that those who miss the session can add their points and also see what other people are asking for prayer about. You can also encourage group members to take the list home and pray again later in the week for each other. But make sure you set some appropriate guidelines for your group about confidentiality when committing prayer points in writing.
- My observation is that men have more trouble thinking of prayer points. So give them some help and focus their thoughts on particular things. For example:
  - Something I need to pray about from the study...
  - A missionary I'd like to pray for...

6   E.g. a shared Google Drive or Dropbox document.

- A workmate I'd like to share the gospel with...
- A family member I'm concerned about...

If you're using the online register idea, you could set up some of these as template prayer points to prompt people.

- Rather than share and pray in a big group, break up into prayer triplets or pairs (keeping them the same for a month at a time to build relationship). Rather than ten people sharing and it taking half an hour, this means two or three people sharing for ten minutes or so, leaving more time to pray—and also less chance someone's prayer points will be forgotten.

- In a big group, ask people to pray, rather than just share, their own prayer points. Although it's nice to have someone else pray about my personal prayer points, if there is a strong sense that my brothers and sisters are praying with me, not much is lost by combining the sharing of prayer points process and the praying into one activity. But make sure there is a hearty 'Amen' said to affirm people in their prayers.

"being watchful in it"

This phrase might remind you a little of the Lord Jesus' instruction to his disciples to "watch and pray" and "stay awake" (Mark 14:38; Luke 21:34-36; Mark 13:32-37). It may have connotations of being watchful for the Lord Jesus' return, but it certainly indicates that we need to be alert to kingdom matters and spiritual dangers—in other words, praying with our eyes wide open. (Not necessarily literally, of course.)

That again should shape the way our home groups pray. As the leader, how are you going to encourage people to pray beyond themselves and their material needs? How do we ensure we pray for wider gospel concerns? And how will your prayers flow out of what God has been saying to you in the passage you have just been studying?

"with thanksgiving"

Focusing our minds on what God has done for us already (as opposed to what we are asking him to do) will inevitably lead us to thanksgiving. So rather than just putting together a list of petitions to present to God, take the time to think and list out ways that God has blessed us—and be sure to thank him for these things. (If you're using the online prayer register document described above, maybe have a section specifically set up for people to add their points of thanksgiving.)

In our brief family prayer times (generally after dinner) we go around the table and quickly share two things: something to give thanks for and something (or someone) to pray for. We find it a helpful practice, and maybe it's one you could use in your home group (or the pairs and triplets in your group).

One final piece of advice: The prayer life of your group will tend to reflect the health of your own personal prayer life as leader. So if this is an area you struggle in, share that struggle with someone (perhaps another home group leader or your pastor) who can help you and pray for you and encourage you to pursue faithfulness in this key area.

Originally published at *GoThereFor.com* and reproduced here with permission. Available online: www.gotherefor.com/offer.php?intid=29767

Praying out loud: some practical tips
By Carmelina Read

It's good for people to pray out loud in our small groups: for encouragement, modelling, and sharing our struggles. What I want to do here is outline a few ideas to help draw people out a little, and help them gain the skills to pray out loud.

Explain Christian prayer

We often take it for granted that everyone knows what Christian prayer is about, but it's now less and less likely that people have had modelled to them what it is to pray to a living God in a personal way with assurance that he hears. It's worth explaining a few fundamentals such as:

- Even though other people are listening to our prayer, we're praying to God. That's why we pray "Dear God".
- The Bible teaches us that through his death and resurrection, Jesus has made it possible for us to pray (Heb 10:19-21) so that's why we close our prayers with something like "In Jesus' name we pray".
- Jesus' death and resurrection have given us access to the throne room of God, so we can be sure God hears our prayers and we can approach God with confidence (Heb 10:19-21). That's why we don't need to impress God with fancy words.
- Because of Jesus, we don't pray to a distant God—we pray to God as our Father (Rom 8:15; Gal 4:6), so we can pray "Dear heavenly Father".

- We close with the word "Amen" as a way of inviting others to affirm our prayers and say they agree. Saying "Amen" at the end of the prayer is also a great way for us to encourage a new person in the group.
- When we pray on our own, we use the word "I". But in a group setting, we're inviting others to pray with us and to say "Amen" to our prayers. So that's why we pray using the word "We". For example, "We pray for June's mum—please help her to recover quickly from her surgery".
- Because we're praying in a group setting, it's important to pray with a clear and fairly loud voice rather than a whisper. This is especially important for people who are used to changing their tone of voice or lowering their voice when they pray. Some people have grown up thinking this is more respectable to God. But whispering makes it hard for others to hear, especially if you have hearing impaired people in your group, mothers with little babies, or you meet in a noisy environment.

You'll be surprised how much more comfortable some people feel to pray out loud once they understand these basic elements of prayer. It's like giving them the club T-shirt so they feel part of the group.

Model short and simple prayers

Jesus warns us not to pray with "empty phrases", "many words", and "long prayers" for pretence, thinking that this is what will impress God (Matt 6:7-8; Mark 12:40). This doesn't mean long prayers are never okay. But it's worth making a conscious effort to model to others that short prayers with simple words are not simply adequate, but heard by God just as much as longer prayers. This is especially important with people who struggle with English, literacy, and concentration (for example, some who are ill or elderly). Long prayers with complicated words or Christian jargon make it very hard for people to understand and follow along. And if that happens, it defeats the purpose of praying out loud together.

Here are some examples of short, simple prayers:

Dear God, thank you for our time together today. Help us believe that your word is living and active. As we study the Bible this morning, give us understanding so that we may love Jesus more and more.

Dear heavenly Father, we praise you that because of Jesus, you forgive us our sin. When we feel like our sin is too bad to be forgiven, help us to remember that Jesus' death is the perfect sacrifice for all our sin.

Naturally, it's hard to always pray at a level that everyone will understand, especially if there are non-Christians or new Christians in our group. Sometimes, this creates opportunities for explanation or to make a time to catch up over a meal or a coffee. But if you know your sheep, then you can cater the prayer times so that they don't feel excluded by lack of understanding, or overcome with anxiety that they can't pray with the 'sophistication' of the rest of the group.

Teaching and praying and speaking in such a way that people can understand is a biblical principle that Paul explains clearly in 1 Corinthians 14. In this chapter, Paul commands the gathering church to conduct their activities in an orderly manner, ensuring one person speaks at a time and that tongues and prophecy must always be interpreted so that the whole church is built up. This is why Paul says that words that are not understandable exclude the outsider and hinder a person from understanding God.

Give people the opportunity to prepare their prayer beforehand

If someone's shy or English isn't their first language, they often find it hard to pray on the spot. Try suggesting they prepare the opening/closing prayer during the week and offer to read it through and help them with their English expression. Make sure you say positive encouraging comments, especially if you do need to correct an aspect of the prayer.

Once someone is willing to pray, it's helpful to ask if praying first will help them feel less nervous. For some people, having to wait until last makes them very anxious.

Prepare a selection of Scripture-based prayers

Write out a few prayers based on the Bible, print them out and ask each member of the group to choose one to pray out loud at the end of your Bible study time. You could also write prayers that reflect the words and teaching of the study you are covering that day.

This method has the added bonus of teaching people to pray scripturally based prayers and to expand what they pray about. Paul's prayers are often long and complex and could be too hard for some in your group. Personally, I find them hard to pray all in one go because his knowledge of God is so deep. But don't abandon Paul's prayers altogether—break them down and paraphrase them if you need to. You could also select one idea at a time.

Here are some examples:

Dear heavenly Father, we bring before you our missionary family, the Griffiths. We pray that the word of the Lord may speed ahead and be honoured as the Griffiths talk to Portuguese people about the gospel of Jesus. We ask all of these things in the name of Jesus. (2 Thess 3:1)

Dear Father in heaven, help us to truly believe that you are always close. Help us not to be anxious about anything. When we're worried, help us to pray to you with thanksgiving in our hearts. As we pray, remind us of the peace we have in Jesus that can calm our hearts and our minds. We ask all of this in the precious name of Jesus. (Phil 4:6-7)

Dear God, your word tells us that when Jesus comes back, he will appear in the clouds of heaven with power and great glory; and that no-one knows when he will return. Please help us to be ready for his return. We pray this in the name of Jesus. (Matt 24:29-44)

Dear Father in heaven, help us to bring honour to Jesus. Help us do good works and understand you better. Please give us your power to keep trusting Jesus and to be joyful, patient and thankful to you. Thank you that you have given us eternal life by taking us away from the rule of Satan and bringing us into the kingdom of your Son by saving us and forgiving us our sins. In Jesus' name we pray. (Col 1:9-14)

Prepare a selection of topics and people to pray about

You could include:

- missionaries by name with their latest prayer points
- the ministry team leaders and leaders of your church
- university ministries and Scripture in schools in your area
- kids' ministry leaders in your church
- non-Christian friends and family by name, asking that they will hear the gospel and have faith in Jesus
- requests for discipline and consistency to draw near to God by reading the Bible and praying every day
- marriages in your church or group
- mission events coming up
- specific sin that people have shared about and need help with
- the development of the fruit of the Spirit—picking one area of growth to focus on (Gal 5:22-23)
- those who are elderly, sick, and grieving in your community or church
- federal, state and local government and our prisons
- Christians around the world who are persecuted for their faith in Jesus
- praise and adoration—don't forget this. Sometimes it's worth asking people to pray 1-2 praise points that start with the words "Dear God, we praise you for being..." or "Dear heavenly Father, we give you praise because Jesus is..."

In my experience, more often than not people don't understand the difference between praise and thanksgiving, so they revert to thanking God for something he has done for us. While thanksgiving is good, it is useful to teach our people to praise God for who he is. Here is an example:

> Dear Father in heaven, we praise you that Jesus is the image of the invisible God, the firstborn of all creation. We give you praise that by him all things were created, in heaven and on earth, visible and invisible, whether thrones or dominions or rulers or authorities—all things were created through him and for him. In Jesus' name we pray. (Col 1:15-16)

Some weeks, you could try printing out a sheet of paper with some topics to pray about or some options of pre-prepared prayers.

————◆————

Originally published at *GoThereFor.com* and reproduced here with permission. Available online: www.gotherefor.com/offer.php?intid=28517

Appendix 9
The discouraging problem of poor attendance
By Ian Carmichael

You've put in the preparation, worked hard at understanding the passage, thought about the study and how you are going to lead the group through it. You are, in other words, primed and ready to go and then... only two of the seven members of your group turn up on the night.

It's hard not to feel dreadfully discouraged, isn't it?

Here are six ideas on how to deal with it.

1. Focus on the positive

Instead of focusing on who isn't there, be glad about the ones you have with you in the room, and thank God for the chance to share his word with them.

The leader of the home group I attend on a Monday night is a great example of this. Every week he welcomes us very warmly and says how much he appreciates us coming along. At the end of the night, he thanks us again for coming and says (genuinely) how much he has enjoyed the time we've spent together. That sort of positive reaction makes me want to keep coming back, and reminds me that he values me being there.

2. Assume good reasons, but not forever

Often people have very valid reasons why they haven't been able to attend: an urgent work obligation, a sick child, transport problems, and many other unavoidable disturbances in the space-time continuum. So don't jump automatically to the conclusion that a group member is just unreliable or slack.

But on the other hand, don't assume good reasons for too long. If someone misses your group, shoot them a text or Facebook message saying: "Missed you Monday night at home group. Everything okay?" It's not pointed or accusatory—just letting people know they were missed. Yet most people will feel like they ought to give you a return message explaining why they weren't there. And that's useful information to a pastoral leader.

If someone misses a couple of group meetings in a row, it's definitely worth a phone call. And, if their reason for missing the group is not a particularly strong one ("I was tired and just didn't feel like it" or "life's really busy at the moment"), it's worth pointing out that when you get tired or busy, your instinct is also to give it a miss. Yet you find that in those periods of life hearing from God's word is really important and having the prayerful concern and support of others is one of the ways God helps you through those times. This is true, of course, but is also a way of pointing out that other people in the group still come when they have those issues.

3. Set expectations in your group

Best done at the beginning of each year is committing together about group expectations in a range of areas (e.g. not talking over or interrupting each other), including the priority we all give to the group. If everyone has agreed upfront, it makes it much easier to deal with the issue through the year. It becomes a simple reminder, either to an individual or to the group as a whole, of the commitment you made to each other.

4. Keep a record

You might actually want to consider keeping track of attendance. We are (I am!) prone to poor recall of who was there and who wasn't, and so can easily exaggerate a problem, or indeed underestimate a problem, in our own minds. So keep a record of who was in the group each week (after everyone has gone!). I wouldn't necessarily recommend bringing to people's attention the fact that you are keeping track ("Hey, did you know your attendance is tracking at 41.5% this year? What's with that?") But tracking attendance is a way of caring.

5. Talk to your church pastor

Sometimes it's worth a quiet word to your pastor about someone's poor attendance. He may know more about the person's situation, or might be in a better position than you to bring it up with them. At the very least, he can join you in prayer and keep an extra eye out for opportunities to minister to the person concerned.

6. Pray about it

I mention this one last not because it is least important, but because it is the one I most want you to remember. Bring the matter to the Lord in prayer, and ask him to prompt the people you are concerned about to come more regularly, and ask him to give you wisdom in knowing what to say to them.

Originally published at *GoThereFor.com* and reproduced here with permission. Available online: www.gotherefor.com/offer.php?intid=28567

Making hard phone calls
By Sandy Grant and Tara Sing

In appendix 9 we discussed the discouraging problem of poor attendance. There are times when poor attendance means as a leader having to make hard calls and chase people up.

It's important that, no matter how awkward, we keep in contact and check in with these occasional attenders. There could be something going on in their lives that may be hindering them from attending. Perhaps they are in need of prayer or some practical love from us. Ultimately, we want to help them to be following Christ and, as Hebrews 10:24-25 says, we want to encourage them to "consider how to stir up one another to love and good works, not neglecting to meet together, as is the habit of some, but encouraging one another..."

Making a follow up phone call to check in with someone who has missed church (or home group) can seem like a daunting thing to do. Below an experienced pastor shares his tips for planning and making that simple (yet sometimes scary) phone call.

Planning the call
Before calling or visiting someone who was absent, consider whether they may have reason to be away (e.g. holidays or illness).

If applicable, it may also be wise to find out if they have been regularly attending their home group/church lately and what their involvement there has been (or perhaps they have been at a different church service or visiting another group that you are unaware of).

Consider various points of contact:

- Church notices and events: Is there anything they missed by being away in the last few weeks, such as a handout or notice or event, that they might be interested in?
- Personal interest: What interests the person who has been absent? What do they like to talk about?
- Social contact: Could you suggest meeting this person for coffee or a meal if they are avoiding church or would benefit from personal attention for some other reason of Christian growth?

Thinking through the above may give you some helpful and caring conversational possibilities.

A sample script

The 'script' provided below is not intended to help you think through *all* of the directions in which a conversation could go. Rather, the goal of this script is to help you provide someone with the opportunity to inform you they were either actually at church or to let you know why they weren't.

Please use your own wording, to match your normal conversational style. You can of course use any other commonsense approach that could help show care for the person or encourage their growth in knowledge and love of Christ.

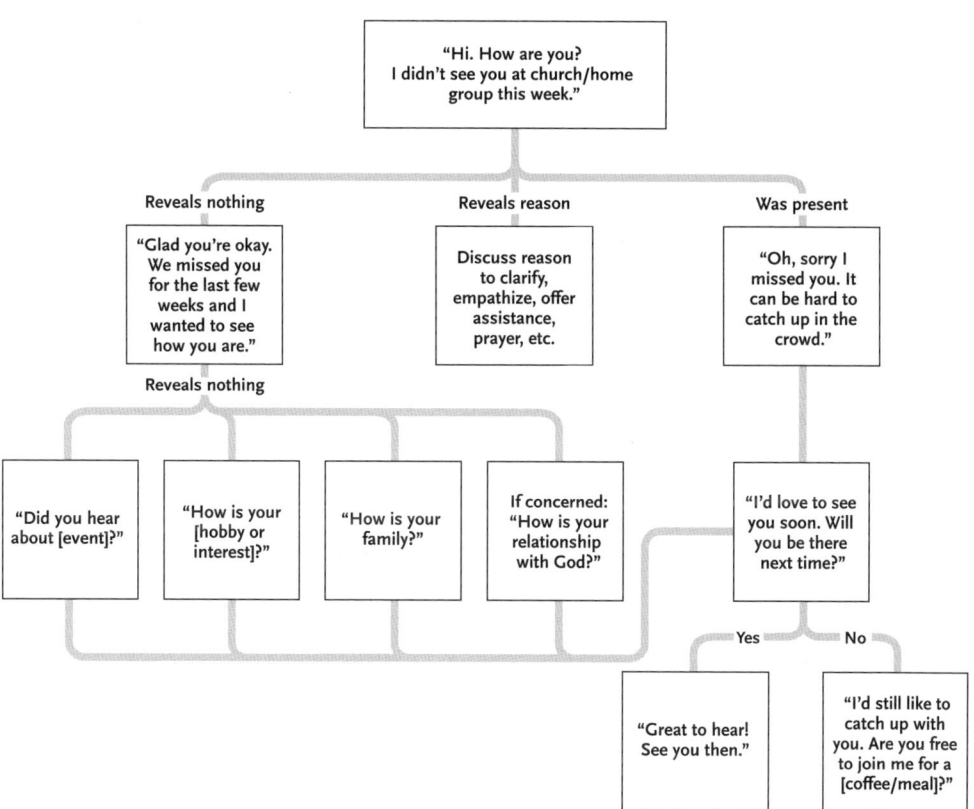

After the call

You may need to stop and organize any further action you promised to undertake for or with them. You might also need to report (with discretion and appropriate regard for confidentiality) any pastoral issues back to a pastoral staff member or another small group leader.

You should also pray for them and keep a special eye out for them at church in the next couple of weeks.

———◆———

Originally published at *GoThereFor.com* and reproduced here with permission. Available online: www.gotherefor.com/offer.php?intid=28571

# matthiasmedia

Matthias Media is an evangelical publishing ministry that seeks to persuade all Christians of the truth of God's purposes in Jesus Christ as revealed in the Bible, and equip them with high-quality resources, so that by the work of the Holy Spirit they will:

- abandon their lives to the honour and service of Christ in daily holiness and decision-making
- pray constantly in Christ's name for the fruitfulness and growth of his gospel
- speak the Bible's life-changing word whenever and however they can—in the home, in the world and in the fellowship of his people.

Our resources range from Bible studies and books through to training courses, audio sermons and children's Sunday School material. To find out more, and to access samples and free downloads, visit our website:

www.matthiasmedia.com

How to buy our resources

1. Direct from us over the internet:
   – in the US: www.matthiasmedia.com
   – in Australia: www.matthiasmedia.com.au

2. Direct from us by phone: please visit our website for current phone contact information.

3. Through a range of outlets in various parts of the world. Visit **www.matthiasmedia.com/contact** for details about recommended retailers in your part of the world.

4. Trade enquiries can be addressed to:
   – in the US and Canada: sales@matthiasmedia.com
   – in Australia and the rest of the world: sales@matthiasmedia.com.au

Register at our website for our **free** regular email update to receive information about the latest new resources, **exclusive special offers**, and free articles to help you grow in your Christian life and ministry.

The Growth Group Notebook
What it is and what it's for

This is not a personal journal. It's a companion for your growth group. It's designed to help your group grow together and grow the gospel together.

Each section aims to focus your collective attention on gospel concerns so that as you study the Bible together, pray together, promote the gospel together, and serve and care for one another, you slowly take on the likeness and fullness of Christ.

In its pages, you can record group prayer points and jot down regular reflections on things God has been teaching you from your times studying the Bible together. But there are also helpful articles on a variety of topics relating to the life of your group, suggestions for broadening the scope of your group prayers, and advice on setting helpful group goals and expectations.

As a bonus, we've also thrown in a section for you to record notes from sermons.

Are you ready to get started?

FOR MORE INFORMATION OR TO ORDER CONTACT:

Matthias Media
Email: sales@matthiasmedia.com.au
www.matthiasmedia.com.au

Matthias Media (USA)
Email: sales@matthiasmedia.com
www.matthiasmedia.com

Being a Small Group Leader

By Richard Sweatman

being a **small group** leader
Richard Sweatman

What makes someone a good small group leader?

A comprehensive knowledge of the Bible? Wisdom that rivals Solomon's? Exceptional people skills? Or is willingness and availability enough?

In *Being a Small Group Leader* Richard Sweatman brings the Bible and his years of small group ministry experience to the task of highlighting five vital areas in which we need to keep growing as Christian leaders:

- Knowledge of God
- Character
- Teaching ability
- Encouragement of others
- Team leadership

Whether you've been leading a small group for days or decades, you'll find warm encouragement to identify areas in which you can improve, and you'll be challenged and helped to make realistic plans for doing so.

This book is also a useful resource for pastors to work through in talking with those who might take up this valuable ministry in the future.

Richard Sweatman has been the maturity pastor at Hunter Bible Church and UniChurch in Newcastle, NSW, for the past 10 years. He spends his time training and equipping leaders in small group ministry.

FOR MORE INFORMATION OR TO ORDER CONTACT:

Matthias Media
Email: sales@matthiasmedia.com.au
www.matthiasmedia.com.au

Matthias Media (USA)
Email: sales@matthiasmedia.com
www.matthiasmedia.com

Writing a Small Group Study

By Richard Sweatman

The Bible study you write for your small group can result in an exhilarating journey that opens God's word up and leads people to grow and change. It can also be a hard slog that seems to have little impact on anyone.

If you're hoping for the former but worried you'll end up with the latter, this book is for you.

Putting together a faithful and illuminating Bible study might seem like a huge task, but in *Writing a Small Group Study* Richard Sweatman breaks that task down into clear and achievable steps that won't overwhelm you. He carefully explains how to work your way through each step to create a study that will engage your small group with God's powerful word.

This book is a superb guide for the new small group leader, as well as an excellent refresher for those who have been leading for years.

Richard Sweatman has been the maturity pastor at Hunter Bible Church and UniChurch in Newcastle, NSW, for the past 10 years. He spends his time training and equipping leaders in small group ministry.

FOR MORE INFORMATION OR TO ORDER CONTACT:

Matthias Media
Email: sales@matthiasmedia.com.au
www.matthiasmedia.com.au

Matthias Media (USA)
Email: sales@matthiasmedia.com
www.matthiasmedia.com